LEARNING
HIRAGANA
AND
KATAKANA

LEARNING HIRAGANA AND KATAKANA

Workbook and Practice Sheets

Tetsuo Takagaki
Kenneth G. Henshall

TUTTLE PUBLISHING
Tokyo • Rutland, Vermont • Singapore

Published by Tuttle Publishing, an imprint of Periplus Editions (HK) Ltd., with editorial offices at 130 Joo Seng Road, #06-01 Singapore 368357 and 364 Innovation Drive, North Clarendon, Vermont 05759 USA.

LCC Card No. 90-70374
ISBN-10: 0-8048-3815-1
ISBN-13: 978-0-8048-3815-3

Previously published in 2005 as *A Guide to Learning Hiragana & Katakana ISBN 0-8048-3391-5*

First edition, 1990

Printed in Singapore

Distributed by:

North America, Latin America and Europe
Tuttle Publishing
364 Innovation Drive,
North Clarendon, VT 05759-9436, USA
Tel: 1 (802) 773 8930
Fax: 1 (802) 773 6993
E-mail: info@tuttlepublishing.com
www.tuttlepublishing.com

Japan
Tuttle Publishing
Yaekari Building, 3rd Floor,
5-4-12 Osaki, Shinagawa-ku,
Tokyo 141-0032
Tel: (81) 3 5437 0171
Fax: (81) 3 5437 0755
E-mail: tuttle-sales@gol.com

Asia Pacific
Berkeley Books Pte Ltd
130 Joo Seng Road #06-01
Singapore 368357
Tel: (65) 6280 1330
Fax: (65) 6280 6290
E-mail: inquiries@periplus.com.sg
www.periplus.com

10 09 08 07   7 6 5 4 3 2

CONTENTS

HOW TO USE THIS BOOK

The main aim of this book is to help students achieve competence in reading and writing *kana,* the phonetic symbols that are fundamental to written Japanese. The book starts with a section entitled An Explanation of *Kana,* which contains everything the student will need to know about the two *kana* systems of *hiragana* and *katakana.* Part I of the workbook section then systematically introduces each *hiragana* symbol, voiced form, and combination, and provides ample practice and review. Part II does the same for *katakana,* while Part III provides an overall review.

The Explanation of *Kana* outlines the function and origin of *kana,* the difference between the two *kana* systems, the various sounds, the combinations, and the conventions of usage. It attempts to be detailed and thorough so that it can be used for reference at any stage. Though all the information about *kana* is grouped together in this one section for ease of reference, it is not expected that the student will read it all before starting on the practice pages. In fact, to do so might give the impression that *kana* are perhaps rather formidable, which is not really the case at all. (Just ask any Japanese child!) We recommend that the student start work on the *hiragana* practice pages after reading the first three subsections — on the function, origin, and basic sounds of *kana.* After finishing practice of the forty-six basic *hiragana* symbols the student should go back to the Explanation and read the subsection on additional sounds, then work through the rest of the *hiragana* practice pages before moving on to the *katakana* practice. The final subsection, on other points to note, is mostly concerned with special *katakana* combinations and can be left until the appropriate point in the *katakana* practice pages, just prior to the final review. Students may modify this order, but we recommend finishing practice of one *kana* system before moving on to the next.

In the practice pages of Parts I and II each *kana* symbol is allotted half a page, permitting plenty of writing practice in the boxes given. We suggest working in pencil, rather than ink, as this will allow for erasing and repeated use. Stroke order and a pronunciation guide are also given for each symbol. In addition, for each symbol there is an illustration of its graphic evolution from its "parent" character (see Explanation of *Kana*) and a reference number for that character as it occurs in *A Guide to Remembering Japanese Characters* (Charles E. Tuttle Company, 1988), together with the character's pronunciation. This may be of interest to readers wishing to continue their studies of written Japanese to an advanced level. (However, some of the original characters are no longer commonly used and therefore are not included in *A Guide to Remembering Japanese Characters.*)

After approximately every ten symbols there are "mini review" pages for further practice, this time using whole words. These are cumulative, containing symbols not only from the group just completed but from earlier groups. The mini reviews can be used purely for copying practice, or, by covering the cue *kana* on the left side of the page, as more challenging writing exercises. They can also be used as vocabulary exercises.

Part III, the Final Review, contains exercises, quizzes, and "do-it-yourself" charts. Unlike the reviews in the first two parts it combines the two *kana* systems, as is natural in Japanese texts. And for a more natural effect the boxes used earlier in the book to help achieve even spacing and proper stroke lengths are dispensed with in this final part.

The words appearing in the reviews have been carefully chosen in keeping with an additional aim of this book, which is to expose readers to key words related to Japanese society and culture. The prime criterion for selecting review words was their suitability for practicing the *kana* symbols, but we thought it would be helpful to students if in addition these words could, whenever possible, have particular relevance to Japanese culture. About half of the 450 or so vocabulary items in the book fall into this category. It is beyond the scope of the book to explain these in detail, but students who take the trouble to find out more about them will be rewarded with a broadened appreciation of Japan's society and culture. In short, we intend that these words should be used as a sort of checklist for an exploration of Japan, rather than simply memorized as isolated vocabulary items.

Readers will occasionally encounter a semicolon between English equivalents given for a Japanese review word. This indicates that the Japanese word is a homophone, that is, a word having a different meaning but the same sound as another. Normally these homophones would be written with different characters, but when expressed in phonetic *kana* script or romanization such differentiation is not possible. The English words separated by a semicolon thus refer to different Japanese words sharing the same *kana* form. (Commas between English words simply indicate nuances of the same word.) It should also be noted that there is sometimes a subtle difference in intonation between "homophones," which cannot be determined from the *kana* or romanization.

Finally, readers are advised to seek specialist or native-speaker guidance on intonation and pronunciation. It should be appreciated that the pronunciation guides given in this book can only ever be approximate, owing to the variety in pronunciation of the same English word in different parts of the world. Also, some Japanese sounds cannot be precisely represented by English letters. The Japanese "r," for example, actually falls between the English "r" and "d." But remember that, with both speaking and writing, practice makes perfect!

AN EXPLANATION OF *KANA*

The Function of *Kana*

Kana are purely phonetic symbols. That is, they are written representations of pronunciation. They can express the entire Japanese language in writing, though in practice the written language uses a mixture of *kana* and *kanji* (characters taken from Chinese).

There are two *kana* systems: *katakana* and *hiragana*. *Katakana* is now mainly used for words taken from languages other than Chinese. *Hiragana* is the more important of the two systems, and is used for everything not written in *katakana* or *kanji*. *Kanji* show meanings of words, though they also have pronunciations. Normally they are used for nouns and the the unchanging part (the stem) of verbs, adjectives, and adverbs, while *hiragana* symbols are used for the changing parts (notably endings). For example, the verb *iku* means "go," while *ikanai* means "not go." The stem is *i-,* and this is usually written with a *kanji,* while the variable endings *-ku* and *-kanai* are written in *hiragana*. *Hiragana* is also used to write particles, and other words where *kanji* are not appropriate. To all intents and purposes the two *kana* systems are not interchangeable, and are rarely mixed within a given word. The rule is: **katakana for non-Chinese loan words, hiragana and kanji for the rest.**

The student of Japanese should ideally aim to learn all the two thousand *kanji* in common use. They play a very practical role in graphically and distinctively conveying the meaning of a written statement, unlike a purely phonetic script, and thereby aid rapid understanding. And naturally, no one can expect to read unedited Japanese texts without a knowledge of *kanji.* However, learning the *kanji* is a time-consuming task. Many of them are structurally complex, and many have a wide range of meanings and pronunciations.

Kana, on the other hand, are much fewer in number, with only forty-six basic symbols in each of the two systems. They are simple to write, and, with very few exceptions, they have fixed pronunciations. If you don't know the *kanji* for a particular word, but know the pronunciation, you can just express that entire word in *kana* (*hiragana,* that is; remember that *katakana* is for non-Chinese foreign words). In other words, while not ideal, **kana (hiragana) can substitute for *kanji*.** This means that even beginners can express themselves in functional written Japanese with relatively little effort.

The Origin of *Kana*

The word *kana* derives from *karina,* meaning "borrowed name," for the *kana* symbols are simplified forms of certain borrowed Chinese characters used for their sound (though, confusingly, the same characters lent their meaning in other contexts). The prefix *hira-* means "ordinary," with connotations of "informal" and "easy," and in this particular case "cursive." Thus *hiragana* means "ordinary (cursive) *kana,*" and indeed *hiragana* has traditionally been the more commonly used of the two systems, and the more cursive. The *hiragana* symbols are simplifications of whole Chinese characters. For example, the *kana* あ (pronounced like the "a" in "car") derives from a cursive rendition of the character 安 (pronounced "an"). *Kata-* means "one side" or "partial," pointing to the fact that *katakana* symbols derive from one part of a Chinese character. For example, イ (pronounced like "ee" in "meet") is the left-hand part of the character 伊 (also pronounced "ee").

Both systems evolved around the end of the eighth century. In those early days *hiragana* was used mostly by women, while men preferred to use the more angular *katakana*. However, these associations have long since disappeared.

The Basic Sounds Represented by *Kana*

Kana symbols basically represent syllables, and the *kana* systems are therefore syllabaries rather than alphabets. Generally the syllables are crisp and clear combinations of one consonant and one following vowel, or one vowel by itself. There is only one consonant that exists as a syllable and *kana* symbol in its own right, *n*.

The use of English letters to refer to Japanese sounds and symbols can produce a number of apparent irregularities. Among other things a combination of consonant and vowel in Japanese will not necessarily have the same pronunciation as in English. For example, while ふ is found in the *h* group (see the table that follows), its pronunciation is actually closer to the English sound "fu" than "hu." To facilitate pronunciation the romanization used in this book is a version of the Hepburn system, which transcribes ふ as *fu* rather than *hu,* but readers should appreciate that there is no direct equivalent in Japanese to an English "f." Similar cases of convenient but seemingly irregular romanization are found in the *s* group and *t* group. This may begin to seem complicated, but in fact correspondence in Japanese between *kana* spelling and pronunciation is much simpler than in the case of English and its alphabet. Attempts to express certain loan words in *katakana* can seem awkward, but that is really a problem relating to the Japanization of non-Japanese words, rather than to the *kana* system itself.

Each of the two *kana* systems contains the same basic forty-six syllables, arranged in the same order. The basic syllabaries are as follows (combined for convenience, with the *kata-kana* written slightly smaller).

VOWELS

		a		i		u		e		o	
		あ	ア a	い	イ i	う	ウ u	え	エ e	お	オ o
	k	か	カ ka	き	キ ki	く	ク ku	け	ケ ke	こ	コ ko
	s	さ	サ sa	し	シ shi	す	ス su	せ	セ se	そ	ソ so
	t	た	タ ta	ち	チ chi	つ	ツ tsu	て	テ te	と	ト to
CONSONANTS	n	な	ナ na	に	ニ ni	ぬ	ヌ nu	ね	ネ ne	の	ノ no
	h	は	ハ ha	ひ	ヒ hi	ふ	フ fu	へ	ヘ he	ほ	ホ ho
	m	ま	マ ma	み	ミ mi	む	ム mu	め	メ me	も	モ mo
	y	や	ヤ ya			ゆ	ユ yu			よ	ヨ yo
	r	ら	ラ ra	り	リ ri	る	ル ru	れ	レ re	ろ	ロ ro
	w	わ	ワ wa							を	ヲ wo
ん	ン n	n										

This order is known as the *gojūonjun,* meaning "the fifty sounds order." In fact, there are now only forty-six basic symbols (sounds) officially in use. *Yi, ye,* and *wu* do not exist. *Wi* (ゐ/ヰ) and *we* (ゑ/ヱ) were officially removed from the list in 1946 since the sounds were considered sufficiently close to *i* and *e* to be represented by the symbols for these. However, the symbols for *wi* and *we* are still encountered on rare occasions.

The *gojūonjun* is the standard order followed by dictionaries and other reference works. It

11

is therefore particularly important to remember it. To this end, the following mnemonic, which is a modified version of one taught by Professors Dunn and O'Neill of the University of London, may be helpful.

Ah, kana signs! Take note how many you read well (n).

The reader will have taken note of the fact that the first letters of these words follow the *gojūonjun* consonant headings. With apologies to mathematicians, even the syllable *n* (ん) is represented, by the mathematical symbol "n" indicating the utmost number (in this case 92, the sum of the two *kana* systems).

The syllable *n* (ん) is sometimes called the "independent n" but in fact it can never be used truly independently. Nor can it ever start a word. When working from romanization it is sometimes difficult to tell whether a non-initial *n* followed by a vowel is a syllable from the *n*- group, or whether it is *n* (ん) followed by an independent vowel. For example, *tani* could be either たに (valley) or たんい (unit). Context usually makes this clear. To avoid ambiguity some romanization systems use an apostrophe after the *n* that represents ん. Thus たんい can be romanized as *tan'i*. Note also that in romanization ん is sometimes written as *m* before a *p, b,* or *m,* as in *shimbun* for *shinbun* (newspaper). This practice is by no means universally followed (and is not followed in this book), but its existence does indicate one of the exceptional cases where the pronunciation of a *kana* symbol could be said to vary slightly according to context.

Additional Sounds Represented by *Kana*

In addition to the forty-six basic symbols, there are sixty-one classified modifications and combinations in each system, and a few further special combinations as well. This may sound alarming, but in fact it involves only a handful of new points to learn.

The first is the *dakuon,* meaning "voiced sound" or "hardened sound." Sounds starting with the unvoiced consonants *k, s, t,* and *h* are voiced as *g, z/j, d/z/j,* and *b* respectively if the diacritical marks ⸌ are added to the upper right side of the basic *kana* symbol, as shown in the following table. (See also pp. 52~56.) The table also shows *handakuon,* meaning "half-voiced sound," which applies only to sounds starting with *h.* The addition of a small circle ○ to the upper right side of the appropriate basic *kana* symbol changes the pronunciation from *h* to *p* (as opposed to changing it to *b* in the case of the full *dakuon*).

	a	i	u	e	o
g	が カ゛ ga	ぎ ギ゛ gi	ぐ グ゛ gu	げ ケ゛ ge	ご ゴ゛ go
z/j	ざ サ゛ za	じ ジ゛ ji	ず ズ゛ zu	ぜ ゼ゛ ze	ぞ ゾ゛ zo
d/z/j	だ ダ゛ da	ぢ チ゛ ji	づ ツ゛ zu	で デ゛ de	ど ド゛ do
b	ば バ゛ ba	び ビ゛ bi	ぶ ブ゛ bu	べ ベ゛ be	ぼ ボ゛ bo
p	ぱ パ° pa	ぴ ピ° pi	ぷ プ° pu	ぺ ペ° pe	ぽ ポ° po

Ji and *zu* are written じ and ず, except when they clearly derive from *chi* (ち) and *tsu* (つ) in compounds or repeated symbols. For example, *hanaji* (nosebleed, from *hana* [nose] and *chi* [blood]) is はなぢ, and *tsuzuku* (continue, from *tsutsuku*) is つづく.

A combination of a consonant and *y-* is known as a *yōon,* meaning "contracted sound." Any of the seven basic consonants *k, s, t, n, h, m,* or *r,* or voiced or half-voiced consonants, can be used. The symbol that represents these consonants plus *i,* for example き *(ki)* or し *(shi),* is followed by a symbol from the *y-* group — either *ya, yu,* or *yo* as appropriate. This second symbol is written smaller, while the *i* sound is barely pronounced and is dropped in romanization. Thus *kyo* is expressed as きょ and *shu* (*syu* in some romanization systems) as しゅ. If the よ or ゆ of our examples were written the same size as the preceding symbols, then they would be treated as uncombined symbols and read *kiyo* or *shiyu* respectively. Full tables are given below. (See also pp. 59~62.)

	a	u	o
ky	きゃ キャ kya	きゅ キュ kyu	きょ キョ kyo
sh	しゃ シャ sha	しゅ シュ shu	しょ ショ sho
ch	ちゃ チャ cha	ちゅ チュ chu	ちょ チョ cho
ny	にゃ ニャ nya	にゅ ニュ nyu	にょ ニョ nyo
hy	ひゃ ヒャ hya	ひゅ ヒュ hyu	ひょ ヒョ hyo
my	みゃ ミャ mya	みゅ ミュ myu	みょ ミョ myo
ry	りゃ リャ rya	りゅ リュ ryu	りょ リョ ryo

	a	u	o
gy	ぎゃ ギャ gya	ぎゅ ギュ gyu	ぎょ ギョ gyo
j	じゃ ジャ ja	じゅ ジュ ju	じょ ジョ jo
j	ぢゃ チ゛ャ ja	ぢゅ チ゛ュ ju	ぢょ チ゛ョ jo

	a	u	o
by	びゃ ビャ bya	びゅ ビュ byu	びょ ビョ byo
py	ぴゃ ピャ pya	ぴゅ ピュ pyu	ぴょ ピョ pyo

Note that ヂ combinations rarely occur.

Some consonants — essentially *k, s, t,* and *p* — can be doubled by inserting a small *tsu* (っ or ッ) in front of them. This combination is known as a *sokuon* (double consonant). Thus *gakki* (school term) is expressed as がっき. The little っ or ッ is not pronounced as such, but the consonant that follows it is given, as it were, a double amount of time for its pronunciation. It is important to apply this extra time to the consonant only, and not to the following vowel. Thus the word in our example should be pronounced *gakki* and not *gakkii.* These double consonants can never begin a word. (See also pp. 57~58.)

Students commonly make the mistake of trying to write a double *n,* as in words like *annai* (guide), with a small っ. The correct way is to use ん to represent the first *n.* Thus *annai* should be written あんない.

The lengthening of vowels (including the vowel sound of syllables in which a consonant precedes the vowel) can also cause errors, especially in the case of the long *o.* In romanization long vowels are usually indicated (if at all) either by writing the vowel twice or by a macron, as in *uu* or *ū* for a long *u.* For loan words in *katakana,* a barlike symbol ― (or │ with vertical script) is used. Thus *rabā* (rubber) is written ラバー. In *hiragana,* the vowels *a, i, u,* and *e* are doubled by simply writing あ, い, う, or え respectively after the preceding symbol. Thus *okāsan* (mother) is written おかあさん. (The doubling of *a* and *e* actually occurs infrequently in *hiragana.* What sounds like a long *e* is usually *e* followed by *i,* as in せんせい, *sensei* [teacher].) A long *o* can sometimes be formed by doubling in the same way as with other vowels, that is, by adding お, but it is more commonly formed by adding う *(u).* Thus *sō* (so, thus) is written そう. The long *o* that takes お was once pronounced slightly differently from the long *o* that takes う, but that is no longer true, and it is necessary to learn each word with a long *o* sound case by case. Fortunately, there are only a few common words that require the addition of お as opposed to う. These include *ōkii* (big, おおきい), *ōi* (many, おおい), *tōi* (far, とおい), *tō* (ten, とお), and *tōri* (way, road, とおり). Students should take particular care not to be misled by the common romanization practice of writing a long *o* as *oo,* when in *hiragana* it is usually お *(o)* plus う *(u).*

Caution is also needed when transcribing from *kana* to romanization. Always check that an apparent long vowel really is a long vowel, and not two unlinked vowels. A typical case of the latter is a verb whose variable ending starts with the same vowel as the last vowel of the stem, or appears to combine with it to make a long *o.* For example, the verb そう, meaning "go with," should always be romanized as *sou* and not *sō* or *soo.* (By contrast, そう meaning "thus," being a genuine long vowel, is romanized as *sō* or *soo.*) Similarly, *suu* is the romanization for the verb すう (suck), rather than *sū,* and *kiite* is the way to romanize the suspensive きいて (listening), rather than *kīte.*

Other Points to Note

There are three common cases where *kana* usage is distinctly irregular. They all involve particles, namely the topic particle *wa*, the object particle *o*, and the directional particle *e* (meaning "to"). These words are written は, を, and へ respectively, and not わ, お, and え as might be expected. The irregularities result from the failure of writing conventions to keep pace with pronunciation changes over the last century or so.

Certain further usages need to be noted with regard to *katakana* loan words only. These are relatively recent attempts to express non-Japanese words with greater accuracy, and tend to be an extension of the *yōon* principle (きょ etc.) seen earlier. That is, they combine two *kana* symbols, the first one lending only its consonant sound and this fact being indicated by the small size of the second symbol. For example, "f" sounds can be approximated by following *fu* (フ) with a small vowel. Thus *fa, fi, fe,* and *fo* are written as ファ, フィ, フェ, and フォ respectively. Similarly, "q" can be represented by *ku* (ク) plus a small vowel, as in クォーター (quarter). A German-style "z" (as in "Mozart") can be shown by *tsu* (ツ) plus a small vowel, i.e., モーツァルト (Mozart). "She" (as in "shepherd"), "che" (as in "check"), and the voiced version "je" are written as シェ, チェ and ジェ. Though not a consonant, *u* (ウ) is used in a similar type of combination, to produce "w" sounds. As mentioned earlier, the sounds *wi* and *we* are still occasionally found expressed by ヰ and ヱ respectively, but nowadays are usually written as ウィ and ウェ. Thus "whisky" (*uisukī*) is usually written as ウィスキー. Theoretically ヲ could be used for *wo*, but this has become so associated with the object particle *o* that ウォ is used instead. (*Wa*, however, is represented by ワ.) In similar fashion, *i* (イ) can be followed by a small エ to express "ye." Thus "Yemen" is イェーメン. Remarkably, an extension of the use of ウ has seen diacritical marks added to it in order to express "v." Thus "Venus" is ヴィーナス. The English sounds "ty" or "ti" (as in "party") and their voiced equivalents "dy" and "di," which were once expressed rather unfaithfully by チ and ジ respectively, are now written as ティ and ディ. Thus "party" is パーティー. The "tu" of "tuba" and the "du" of "due" can be expressed by テュ and デュ, giving テューバ (tuba) and デュエット (duet), while the "Tou" of "Toulouse" can be shown by トゥ (a voiced version is also possible).

These combinations have very recently received official approval, particularly when used in proper nouns such as place names and personal names. However, there is also official recognition of established usage, such as of *b* for *v*. This means that in practice some words can be written in a number of ways. "Violin" can be either ヴァイオリン or バイオリン, for example. In cases where a certain usage has become particularly firmly entrenched in the Japanese language the old rendition is favored, such as ミルクセーキ (mirukusēki) for

15

"milkshake" (but note that "Shakespeare" is シェークスピア). At the same time, it is also possible to make up new combinations as appropriate, such as 二 *(ni)* plus a small エ *(e)* to express the *nye* sound of the Russian *nyet*. In short, the student should be prepared for a range of creative and sometimes inconsistent usages.

Katakana is very occasionally used for words other than loan words. For example, it can be used to emphasize or highlight words, such as entries in academic reference works, and is also used in telegrams and certain military and official documents. In such cases, when used for purely Japanese or Chinese-derived words, its conventions of usage are identical to those of *hiragana*. Long vowels, for instance, are formed by adding the appropriate vowel and not by a bar. Thus *gakkō* (school) is ガッコウ, rather than ガッコー.

A *kana* symbol can be repeated by the special symbol ゝ. This can also be used when the second symbol is a voiced version of the first, in which case it becomes ゞ. Where more than one syllable is repeated, in vertical script only, 〱 (or 〲 if the first of the repeated sounds is voiced) can be used, with the symbol covering two spaces. These repetition symbols are known collectively as *odoriji* (jump symbols). Students need to recognize them, but should only use them, if at all, with caution. They are not compulsory, and have a number of restrictions on their usage. For example, they cannot be used where the first symbol of one word is the same as the last symbol of the word that precedes it (as in *kuroi ishi* meaning "black stone"), or similarly in compound words where the first symbol of the second word coincides with the last symbol of the first word (as in *tama-matsuri* meaning "festival of the dead"), or where the first symbol of a variable word ending is the same as the last symbol of the word stem (as in *ki-kimasu* meaning "listen"). Some examples of correct usage:

mimi	*kagami*	*iroiro*	*samazama*
(ear)	(mirror)	(various)	(various)

Finally, students should learn the basic Japanese punctuation marks, known as *kutōten*. Full stops are written 。 *(maru)*, and commas are written 、 *(ten)*. Quotation marks *(kagi)*, are written 「 」 in horizontal script and in vertical script.

I

HIRAGANA

ORIGIN (AN 223)

| 安 | あ | あ | あ |

STROKE ORDER

| 一 | 十 | あ | |

あ

a

as "a" in "car," but shorter

PRACTICE

| あ | あ | あ | あ | あ | あ | あ | あ | あ | あ |
| あ | あ | あ | あ | あ | あ | あ | あ | あ | あ |

ORIGIN (I 419)

| 以 | ん | いろ | い |

STROKE ORDER

| し | い | | |

い

i

as "ee" in "meet," but shorter

PRACTICE

| い | い | い | い | い | い | い | い | い | い |
| い | い | い | い | い | い | い | い | い | い |

う

u

as "u" in "hula," but shorter

ORIGIN (U 811)

宇	宁	ら	う

STROKE ORDER

ヽ	う		

PRACTICE

え

e

as "e" in "get"

ORIGIN (E/I 420)

衣	え	え	え

STROKE ORDER

ヽ	ゔ	え	

PRACTICE

ORIGIN   (O)

| 於 | わ | ぬ | お |

STROKE ORDER

| ー | あ | お | |

お

o

as "o" in "or," but shorter

PRACTICE

| お | お | お | お | お | お | お | お | お | お |
| お | お | お | お | お | お | お | お | お | お |

ORIGIN   (KA 431)

| 加 | かい | か | か |

STROKE ORDER

| つ | カ | か | |

か

ka

as "ca" in "car," but shorter

PRACTICE

| か | か | か | か | か | か | か | か | か | か |
| か | か | か | か | か | か | か | か | か | か |

き

ki

as "ki" in "keep," but shorter

ORIGIN   (KI 1129)

幾	岑	き	き

STROKE ORDER

一	二	き	き

PRACTICE

く

ku

as "Ku" in "Kuwait," but shorter

ORIGIN   (KU 647)

久	乆	く	く

STROKE ORDER

く			

PRACTICE

ORIGIN   (KEI 105)

計	汁	け	け

STROKE ORDER

l	l‐	け	

け

ke

as "ke" in "keg"

PRACTICE

け	け	け	け	け	け	け	け	け	け
け	け	け	け	け	け	け	け	け	け

ORIGIN   (KO 855)

己	己	己	こ

STROKE ORDER

⁓	こ		

こ

ko

as "co" in "core," but shorter

PRACTICE

こ	こ	こ	こ	こ	こ	こ	こ	こ	こ
こ	こ	こ	こ	こ	こ	こ	こ	こ	こ

MINI REVIEW あ—こ / A—KO

ai   love

あい　あい　あい　あい　あい　あい　あい

ue   above, top

うえ　うえ　うえ　うえ　うえ　うえ　うえ

oka   hill

おか　おか　おか　おか　おか　おか　おか

kiku   hear, ask; chrysanthemum

きく　きく　きく　きく　きく　きく　きく

koke   moss

こけ　こけ　こけ　こけ　こけ　こけ　こけ

ike   pond

いけ　いけ　いけ　いけ　いけ　いけ　いけ

kau   buy

かう　かう　かう　かう　かう　かう　かう

eki   station

えき　えき　えき　えき　えき　えき　えき

iku   go

いく　いく　いく　いく　いく　いく　いく

koko   here

ここ　ここ　ここ　ここ　ここ　ここ　ここ

au   meet

あう　あう　あう　あう　あう　あう　あう

koe — voice

こえ

kaku — write

かく

oke — wooden bucket

おけ

kao — face, honor

かお

ie — house, extended family

いえ

aki — autumn

あき

iu — say

いう

akai — red

あかい

aoi — blue

あおい

kioku — memory

きおく

ekaki — painter

えかき

sa

as "sa" in "sarcasm," but shorter

ORIGIN   (SA 22)

左　き　と　さ

STROKE ORDER

一　さ　さ

PRACTICE

shi

as "shee" in "sheep," but shorter

ORIGIN   (SHI, part of 1335)

え　え　し　し

STROKE ORDER

し

PRACTICE

ORIGIN   (SUN 909)

すすすす

STROKE ORDER

一　す

PRACTICE

す す す す す す す す す す
す す す す す す す す す す

su

as "Su" in "Susan," but shorter

ORIGIN   (SE 327)

世をセせ

STROKE ORDER

一　十　せ

PRACTICE

せ せ せ せ せ せ せ せ せ せ
せ せ せ せ せ せ せ せ せ せ

se

as "se" in "set"

そ

so

as "so" in "sore," but shorter

ORIGIN (SO, part of ZŌ 741)

STROKE ORDER

PRACTICE

た

ta

as "ta" in "tar," but shorter

ORIGIN (TA 164)

STROKE ORDER

PRACTICE

ORIGIN   (CHI 169)

知 ち ち ち

STROKE ORDER

一 ち

ち

chi

as "chee" in "cheek," but shorter

PRACTICE

ち ち ち ち ち ち ち ち ち ち
ち ち ち ち ち ち ち ち ち ち

ORIGIN   (SU 304)

州 以 ツ つ

STROKE ORDER

つ

つ

tsu

as "tsu" in "tsunami"

PRACTICE

つ つ つ つ つ つ つ つ つ つ
つ つ つ つ つ つ つ つ つ つ

29

て

te

as "te" in "ten"

ORIGIN   (TEN 58)

STROKE ORDER

PRACTICE

と

to

as "to" in "tore," but shorter

ORIGIN   (TO-maru 129)

STROKE ORDER

PRACTICE

MINI REVIEW さ － と / SA － TO

sushi   sushi

すし　すし　すし　すし　すし　すし　すし

tsuchi   soil

つち　つち　つち　つち　つち　つち　つち

soto   outside

そと　そと　そと　そと　そと　そと　そと

sake   saké; salmon

さけ　さけ　さけ　さけ　さけ　さけ　さけ

tetsu   iron, steel

てつ　てつ　てつ　てつ　てつ　てつ　てつ

seki   seat; cough

せき　せき　せき　せき　せき　せき　せき

tatsu   stand, leave; dragon

たつ　たつ　たつ　たつ　たつ　たつ　たつ

tochi   land

とち　とち　とち　とち　とち　とち　とち

uta   song, poem

うた　うた　うた　うた　うた　うた　うた

koto   thing; Japanese harp

こと　こと　こと　こと　こと　こと　こと

suso   hem

すそ　すそ　すそ　すそ　すそ　すそ　すそ

tai sea bream

たい

teki enemy

てき

shichi seven

しち

ase sweat

あせ

sasu thrust; indicate

さす

uso untruth

うそ

kisetsu season

きせつ

ashita tomorrow

あした

satoi clever, sharp (of senses)

さとい

sekitei rock garden (Japanese style)

せきてい

chikatetsu subway

ちかてつ

ORIGIN (NA)

奈	ち	ち	な

STROKE ORDER

一	ナ	た	な

な

na

as "na" in "narcotic," but shorter

PRACTICE

ORIGIN (NI 906)

仁	仁	に	に

STROKE ORDER

l	に	に	

に

ni

as "nea" in "neat," but shorter

PRACTICE

33

nu

as "noo" in "noon," but shorter

ORIGIN (NU/DO 1638)

STROKE ORDER

PRACTICE

ne

as "ne" in "net"

ORIGIN (NE)

STROKE ORDER

PRACTICE

の

ORIGIN   (NO/NAI)

乃　乃　乃　の

STROKE ORDER

の

PRACTICE

no

as "no" in "north,"
but shorter

は

ORIGIN   (HA 367)

波　波　は　は

STROKE ORDER

し　し　は

PRACTICE

ha

as "ha" in "harm,"
but shorter

35

ひ

hi

as "hea" in "heat," but shorter

ORIGIN   (HI 771)

STROKE ORDER

PRACTICE

ふ

fu

as "foo" in "fool," but with softer "f"

ORIGIN   (FU 572)

STROKE ORDER

PRACTICE

ORIGIN   (HE/BU 384)

| 部 | ろ | つ | へ |

へ

he

as "he" in "hen"

STROKE ORDER

| へ | | | |

PRACTICE

ORIGIN   (HO 787)

| 保 | 泓 | ほ | ほ |

ほ

ho

as "ho" in "horn," but shorter

STROKE ORDER

| l | lー | lー | ほ |

PRACTICE

37

MINI REVIEW な—ほ / NA — HO

nani   what

な に

hone   bone

ほ ね

nuno   cloth

ぬ の

hifu   skin

ひ ふ

heta   clumsy

へ た

hana   flower, blossom; nose

は な

fune   boat

ふ ね

kani   crab

か に

hina   doll, fledgling

ひ な

hashi   chopsticks; bridge; edge

は し

kinu   silk

き ぬ

hoshi   star

ほ し

hito   person

ひ と

noki   eaves

の き

nishi   west

に し

haiku   haiku

は い く

katana   curved sword

か た な

netsuke   carved figurine

ね つ け

tanuki   raccoon dog

た ぬ き

seifu   government

せ い ふ

inoshishi   wild boar

い の し し

heisotsu   soldier

へ い そ つ

ま

ma

as "ma" in "mark," but shorter

ORIGIN (MATSU 587)

STROKE ORDER

PRACTICE

み

mi

as "mea" in "meat," but shorter

ORIGIN (BI 376)

STROKE ORDER

PRACTICE

ORIGIN   (MU 781)

武　あ　む　む

STROKE ORDER

一　む　む

む

mu

as "moo" in "moon," but shorter

PRACTICE

ORIGIN   (ME 35)

女　女　め　め

STROKE ORDER

丶　め

め

me

as "me" in "met"

PRACTICE

41

mo

as "mo" in "more," but shorter

ORIGIN   (MŌ 210)

STROKE ORDER

PRACTICE

ya

as "ya" in "yard," but shorter

ORIGIN   (YA, part of CHI 167)

STROKE ORDER

PRACTICE

ORIGIN   (YU 399)

由 申 由 ゆ

STROKE ORDER

い ゆ

PRACTICE

ゆ

yu

as "you" in "youth," but shorter

ORIGIN   (YO 1873)

与 与 よ よ

STROKE ORDER

一 よ

PRACTICE

yo

as "Yo" in "York," but shorter

43

MINI REVIEW ま — よ / MA — YO

yama — mountain, hill

やま

yume — dream

ゆめ

yomu — read

よむ

momo — peach

もも

miya — shrine

みや

kome — uncooked rice

こめ

tsuyu — dew

つゆ

mushi — insect

むし

matsu — pine; wait

まつ

ume — Japanese plum

うめ

mune — chest, breast

むね

kimono kimono, clothing

きもの

sashimi sliced raw fish

さしみ

Yamato old name for Japan

やまと

yukata cotton kimono

ゆかた

sumie India-ink drawing

すみえ

emaki picture scroll

えまき

hanami blossom viewing

はなみ

mikoshi portable shrine

みこし

ukiyoe woodblock print

うきよえ

setomono porcelain

せともの

sukiyaki sukiyaki

すきやき

45

ら

ra

as "ra" in "mirage," but shorter

ORIGIN (RA/RYŌ 598)

良	ら	ら	ら

STROKE ORDER

`	ら		

PRACTICE

り

ri

as "ree" in "reek," but shorter

ORIGIN (RI 596)

利	わ	り	り

STROKE ORDER

い	り		

PRACTICE

ORIGIN   (RU 805)

留 るるる

STROKE ORDER

る

PRACTICE

る

ru

as "ru" in "rule,"
but shorter

ORIGIN   (REI 413)

礼 礼 れ れ

STROKE ORDER

| れ

PRACTICE

れ

re

as "re" in "red"

ろ

ro

as "ro" in "roar," but shorter

ORIGIN   (RO 256)

呂	呂	ろ	ろ

STROKE ORDER

ろ			

PRACTICE

ろ								

わ

wa

as "wa" in "watt"

ORIGIN   (WA 416)

和	和	わ	わ

STROKE ORDER

	わ		

PRACTICE

わ								

ORIGIN   (ON/EN 79)

遠 を あ を

STROKE ORDER

一 ち を

PRACTICE

を

o

as "o" in "or," but shorter

ORIGIN   (MU)

无 ん ん ん

STROKE ORDER

ん

PRACTICE

ん

n

as "n" in "sin"

MINI REVIEW ら—ん / RA — N

wan   bowl; bay

わん

tera   temple

てら

tsuru   crane; to fish

つる

kore   this

これ

furo   bath

ふろ

nori   edible seaweed; paste

のり

haru   spring; to stretch

はる

rei   politeness; soul; example

れい

shiro   castle; white

しろ

Nihon   Japan

にほん

sakura   cherry blossom

さくら

MINI REVIEW ら—ん / RA — N

uchiwa　　　　round fan

うちわ

matsuri　　　　festival

まつり

hotaru　　　　firefly

ほたる

futon　　　　futon

ふとん

rekishi　　　　history

れきし

wafuku　　　　Japanese clothing

わふく

riron　　　　theory

りろん

furoshiki　　cloth wrapper for parcels

ふろしき

harakiri　　harakiri

はらきり

Hinomaru　Rising Sun Flag

ひのまる

samurai　　samurai

さむらい

VOICED AND HALF-VOICED SOUNDS

ga   as "ga" in "garden" but shorter

か゛													

gi   as "gee" in "geese" but shorter

き゛													

gu   as "goo" in "goose" but shorter

く゛													

ge   as "ge" in "get"

け゛													

go   as "go" in "gore" but shorter

こ゛													

za   as "za" in "bizarre" but shorter

さ゛													

ji   as "jee" in "jeep" but shorter

じ													

zu   as "zoo" but shorter

す゛													

ze   as "ze" in "zest"

せ゛													

zo   as "zo" in "Azores" but shorter

そ゛													

da   as "da" in "dark" but shorter

だ												

ji   as "jee" in "jeep" but shorter

ぢ												

zu   as "zoo" but shorter

づ												

de   as "de" in "desk"

で												

do   as "doo" in "door" but shorter

ど												

ba   as "ba" in "bark" but shorter   **pa**   as "pa" in "park" but shorter

ば					ぱ							

bi   as "bea" in "beak" but shorter **pi**   as "pea" in "peak" but shorter

び					ぴ							

bu   as "boo" in "boot" but shorter **pu**   as "poo" in "pool" but shorter

ぶ					ぷ							

be   as "be" in "beg"   **pe**   as "pe" in "peg"

べ					ぺ							

bo   as "bo" in "bore" but shorter **po**   as "po" in "pork" but shorter

ぼ					ぽ							

REVIEW OF VOICED AND HALF-VOICED SOUNDS

obi   waist sash for kimono

おび

fude   writing brush

ふで

Zen   Zen

ぜん

soba   buckwheat noodles; side

そば

biwa   lute; loquat

びわ

geta   wooden clogs

げた

Obon   Buddhist festival

おぼん

Kabuki   Kabuki drama

かぶき

ojigi   bow (head)

おじぎ

sanpo   walk, stroll

さんぽ

monpe   old-style work pants

もんぺ

keigo   polite language

けいご

mikado   old word for emperor

みかど

manga   cartoon

まんが

mikuji   written oracle

みくじ

yakuza   gangster

やくざ

nigiri   rice ball

にぎり

tengu   long-nosed goblin

てんぐ

hanaji   nosebleed

はなぢ

mizuwari   whisky and water

みずわり

zonjiru   know, believe

ぞんじる

daibutsu   large statue of Buddha

だいぶつ

kamikaze kamikaze

かみかぜ

origami origami

おりがみ

senpai senior

せんぱい

bonsai bonsai

ぼんさい

ikebana ikebana

いけばな

enpitsu pencil

えんぴつ

yokozuna sumo grand champion

よこづな

tenpura tempura

てんぷら

senbei rice cracker

せんべい

hanafuda flower cards (game)

はなふだ

Fujisan Mt. Fuji

ふじさん

REVIEW OF DOUBLE VOWELS AND CONSONANTS

ā (aa)   like that; Oh!

あ あ

ii   good

い い

ē (ee)   yes

え え

kū   sky, void, nothingness

く う

kuu   eat

く う

tō   ten

と お

tō   tower, pagoda

と う

tou   ask

と う

kappa   mythical creature

か っ ぱ

shikki   lacquerware

し っ き

sumō   sumo

す も う

57

zōri   sandals

ぞ　う　り

sūji   numeral

す　う　じ

yūgen   tranquil beauty

ゆ　う　げ　ん

gakkō   school

が　っ　こ　う

kōyō   red leaves

こ　う　よ　う

ōkii   big

お　お　き　い

kendō   kendo

け　ん　ど　う

jingū   shrine

じ　ん　ぐ　う

fūrin   wind chime

ふ　う　り　ん

shintō   Shinto

し　ん　ど　う

kūkō   airport

く　う　こ　う

COMBINED SOUNDS KYA—RYO / きゃ－りょ

kya

きゃ

kyu

きゅ

kyo

きょ

sha

しゃ

shu

しゅ

sho

しょ

cha

ちゃ

chu

ちゅ

cho

ちょ

nya

にゃ

nyu

にゅ

nyo

にょ

hya

ひゃ

hyu

ひゅ

hyo

ひょ

mya

みゃ

myu

みゅ

myo

みょ

rya

りゃ

ryu

りゅ

ryo

りょ

VOICED COMBINED SOUNDS GYA—BYO / ぎゃ — びょ

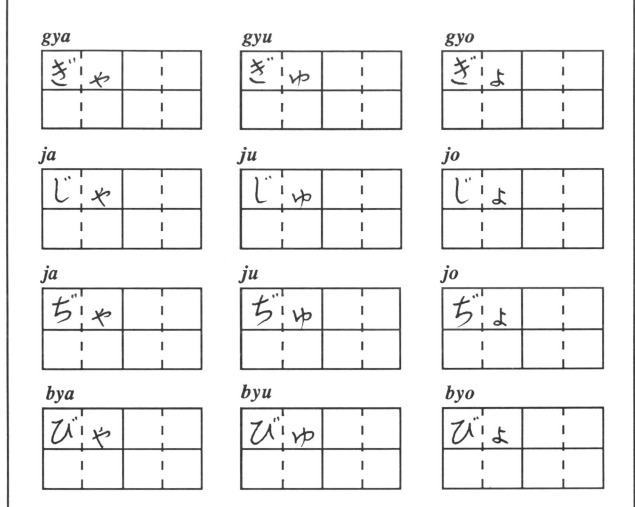

gya

ぎゃ

gyu

ぎゅ

gyo

ぎょ

ja

じゃ

ju

じゅ

jo

じょ

ja

ぢゃ

ju

ぢゅ

jo

ぢょ

bya

びゃ

byu

びゅ

byo

びょ

HALF-VOICED COMBINED SOUNDS PYA—PYO / ぴゃ — ぴょ

pya

ぴゃ

pyu

ぴゅ

pyo

ぴょ

REVIEW OF COMBINED SOUNDS

kyaku   guest, visitor

きゃく

shōji   sliding screen

しょうじ

byōbu   folding screen

びょうぶ

jinja   shrine

じんじゃ

chanoyu   tea ceremony

ちゃのゆ

geisha   geisha

げいしゃ

shodō   calligraphy

しょどう

yakyū   baseball

やきゅう

enryo   reserve, restraint

えんりょ

myōji   family name

みょうじ

kingyo   goldfish

きんぎょ

nyūshi   entrance examination

にゅうし

Jukyō   Confucianism

じゅきょう

chōchin   paper lantern

ちょうちん

hyōzan   iceberg

ひょうざん

ryūgaku   overseas study

りゅうがく

kōjō   factory

こうじょう

jūdō   judo

じゅうどう

Bukkyō   Buddhism

ぶっきょう

shōgun   shogun

じょうぐん

nyōbō   wife

にょうぼう

happyō   announcement

はっぴょう

REVIEW THROUGH PLACE NAMES AND PERIOD NAMES

Nara place, period 710 - 794

な　ら

Edo place, period 1603 - 1868

え　ど

Kōbe place

こ　う　べ

Yayoi period c. 250 B.C. - c. A.D. 250

や　よ　い

Ginza place

ぎ　ん　ざ

Hakone place

は　こ　ね

Meiji period 1868 - 1912

め　い　じ

Nagoya place

な　ご　や

Matsushima place

ま　つ　し　ま

Heian period 794 - 1185

へ　い　あ　ん

Shōwa period 1926 - 1989

し　ょ　う　わ

Nikkō　　place

にっこう

Sapporo　　place

さっぽろ

Ōsaka　　place

おおさか

Kyōto　　place

きょうと

Muromachi　　period 1392 - 1573

むろまち

Heisei　　period 1989 -

へいせい

Kamakura　　period 1185 - 1333

かまくら

Honshū　　place

ほんしゅう

Taishō　　period 1912 - 1926

たいしょう

Jōmon　　period c. 8000 - c. 250 B.C.

じょうもん

Tōkyō　　place

とうきょう

GENERAL REVIEW

Nō　　　　　　Noh

のう

sabi　　　　　　elegant simplicity; rust

さび

semi　　　　　　cicada

せみ

giri　　　　　　duty, honor

ぎり

tako　　　　　　kite; octopus

たこ

hakama　　　　　　divided skirt

はかま

urushi　　　　　　lacquer

うるし

honne　　　　　　one's real intent

ほんね

kokeshi　　　　　　stylized wooden doll

こけし

haniwa　　　　　　clay figurine

はにわ

udon　　　　　　wheat noodles

うどん

kotatsu — brazier, footwarmer

こたつ

amae — childlike dependence

あまえ

Ebisu — name of god of wealth

えびす

miai — interview for marriage

みあい

tōfu — tofu

とうふ

seibo — year-end gift

せいぼ

shibumi — astringency

しぶみ

aware — pathos

あわれ

gohan — meal, cooked rice

ごはん

gagaku — ancient court music

ががく

noren — shop curtain

のれん

haori   short coat

はおり

meishi   name card

めいし

odori   dance

おどり

kaisha   company

かいしゃ

menboku   reputation, "face"

めんぼく

shinju   pearl

しんじゅ

mugicha   barley tea

むぎちゃ

tennō   emperor

てんのう

shōgi   Japanese chess

しょうぎ

onsen   hot spring

おんせん

misoshiru   miso soup

みそしる

67

ninja   ninja

に ん じ ゃ

tokonoma   decorative alcove

と こ の ま

soroban   abacus

そ ろ ば ん

bunraku   puppet theater

ぶ ん ら く

bentō   box lunch

べ ん と う

dantai   group

だ ん た い

shamisen   samisen

し ゃ み せ ん

Shōgatsu   New Year

し ょ う が つ

shakuhachi   flute

し ゃ く は ち

koinobori   carp streamer

こ い の ぼ り

janken   "scissors-paper-stone" game

じ ゃ ん け ん

II

KATAKANA

ORIGIN   (A)

阿	β	ア	ア

STROKE ORDER

⁻	ア		

ア

a

as "a" in "car," but shorter

PRACTICE

ア									

ORIGIN   (I)

伊	イ		

STROKE ORDER

ノ	イ		

イ

i

as "ee" in "meet," but shorter

PRACTICE

イ									

ウ

u

as "u" in "hula," but shorter

ORIGIN (U 811)

宇	ウ	ウ	ウ

STROKE ORDER

'	''	ウ	

PRACTICE

エ

e

as "e" in "get"

ORIGIN (E 1244)

江	讠工	工	エ

STROKE ORDER

一	丁	エ	

PRACTICE

ORIGIN   (O)

| 於 | 方 | オ | オ |

STROKE ORDER

| 一 | 才 | オ | |

オ

o

as "o" in "or," but shorter

PRACTICE

ORIGIN   (KA 431)

| 加 | か | カ | カ |

STROKE ORDER

| フ | カ | | |

カ

ka

as "ca" in "car," but shorter

PRACTICE

キ

ki

as "ki" in "keep,"
but shorter

ORIGIN   (KI 1129)

幾	き	キ	キ

STROKE ORDER

一	二	キ	

PRACTICE

ク

ku

as "Ku" in "Kuwait,"
but shorter

ORIGIN   (KU 647)

久	ス	ク	ク

STROKE ORDER

ノ	ク		

PRACTICE

74

ORIGIN   (KAI 1059)

介 个 ケ ケ

ケ

ke

as "ke" in "keg"

STROKE ORDER

ノ ト ケ

PRACTICE

ORIGIN   (KO 855)

己 己 コ コ

コ

ko

as "co" in "core," but shorter

STROKE ORDER

フ コ

PRACTICE

サ

sa

as "sa" in "sarcasm," but shorter

ORIGIN   (SAN 492)

散 苏 サ サ

STROKE ORDER

一 十 サ

PRACTICE

シ

shi

as "shee" in "sheep," but shorter

ORIGIN   (SHI, part of 1335)

え ミ レ シ

STROKE ORDER

ヽ ミ シ

PRACTICE

ORIGIN (SU)

須 級 ス ス

ス

su

as "Su" in "Susan," but shorter

STROKE ORDER

フ ス

PRACTICE

ORIGIN (SE 327)

世 せ セ セ

セ

se

as "se" in "set"

STROKE ORDER

フ セ

PRACTICE

ソ

so

as "so" in "sore," but shorter

ORIGIN   (SO, part of ZŌ 741)

曾	そ	＼	ソ

STROKE ORDER

＼	ソ		

PRACTICE

タ

ta

as "ta" in "tar," but shorter

ORIGIN   (TA 163)

多	夕		

STROKE ORDER

ノ	ク	夕	

PRACTICE

ORIGIN   (CHI 47)

千 | チ | |

STROKE ORDER

丿 | 二 | 千 |

千

chi

as "chee" in "cheek,"
but shorter

PRACTICE

ORIGIN   (SU 304)

州 | 州 | ツ | ツ

STROKE ORDER

丶 | ⺀ | ツ |

ツ

tsu

as "tsu" in "tsunami"

PRACTICE

テ

te

as "te" in "ten"

ORIGIN   (TEN 58)

| 天 | 天 | 于 | テ |

STROKE ORDER

| 一 | 二 | テ | |

PRACTICE

ト

to

as "to" in "tore," but shorter

ORIGIN   (TO-maru 129)

| 止 | 止 | ト | ト |

STROKE ORDER

| 丨 | ト | | |

PRACTICE

MINI REVIEW アート /A —TO

katsu — cutlet

カ ツ

aisu — ice

ア イ ス

ēsu — ace

エ ー ス

kēki — cake

ケ ー キ

auto — out (baseball)

ア ウ ト

sāchi — search

サ ー チ

kōto — coat; court (sports)

コ ー ト

tsuā — tour

ツ ア ー

tesuto — test

テ ス ト

shītsu — sheet (bed)

シ ー ツ

sekuto — sect

セ ク ト

kōchi — coach (sports)

コ ー チ

sōsu — sauce

ソ ー ス

sukī — ski, skiing

ス キ ー

takushī — taxi

タ ク シ ー

sutēki — steak

ス テ ー キ

sētā — sweater

セ ー タ ー

sākasu — circus

サ ー カ ス

ōkē — okay

オ ー ケ ー

ēkā — acre

エ ー カ ー

akashia — acacia

ア カ シ ア

sukēto — skate, skating

ス ケ ー ト

ORIGIN   (NA)

ナ

na

as "na" in "narcotic," but shorter

STROKE ORDER

PRACTICE

ORIGIN   (NI 61)

ニ

ni

as "nea" in "neat," but shorter

STROKE ORDER

PRACTICE

又

nu

as "noo" in "noon," but shorter

ORIGIN   (NU/DO 1638)

| 奴 | 又 | 又 | 又 |

STROKE ORDER

| フ | 又 | | |

PRACTICE

ネ

ne

as "ne" in "net"

ORIGIN   (NE)

| 禰 | 祢 | ネ | ネ |

STROKE ORDER

| ﾉ | ウ | ネ | ネ |

PRACTICE

ORIGIN   (NO/NAI)

STROKE ORDER

PRACTICE

no

as "no" in "north,"
but shorter

ORIGIN   (HACHI 66)

STROKE ORDER

PRACTICE

ha

as "ha" in "harm,"
but shorter

ヒ

hi

as "hea" in "heat," but shorter

ORIGIN   (HI 771)

比	ひ	ヒ	ヒ

STROKE ORDER

一	ヒ		

PRACTICE

ヒ									

フ

fu

as "foo" in "fool," but with softer "f"

ORIGIN   (FU 572)

不	フ	フ	

STROKE ORDER

フ			

PRACTICE

フ									

ORIGIN   (HE/BU 384)

| 部 | ろ | ヘ | ヘ |

STROKE ORDER

| ヘ | | | |

ヘ

he

as "he" in "hen"

PRACTICE

ORIGIN   (HO 787)

| 保 | 尒 | ホ | |

STROKE ORDER

| 一 | 十 | オ | ホ |

ホ

ho

as "ho" in "horn," but shorter

PRACTICE

87

ma

as "ma" in "mark," but shorter

ORIGIN   (MATSU 587)

STROKE ORDER

PRACTICE

mi

as "mea" in "meat," but shorter

ORIGIN   (MI 23)

STROKE ORDER

PRACTICE

ORIGIN   (MU)

牟 ム ム

STROKE ORDER

ㄥ ム

ム

mu

as "moo" in "moon," but shorter

PRACTICE

ORIGIN   (ME 35)

女 女 乂 乂

STROKE ORDER

ノ メ

メ

me

as "me" in "met"

PRACTICE

モ

mo

as "mo" in "more," but shorter

ORIGIN (MŌ 210)

毛	モ	モ	モ

STROKE ORDER

一	二	モ	

PRACTICE

モ									

ヤ

ya

as "ya" in "yard," but shorter

ORIGIN (YA, part of CHI 167)

也	セ	セ	ヤ

STROKE ORDER

ウ	ヤ		

PRACTICE

ヤ									

ORIGIN   (YU 399)

由	ユ	ユ	

STROKE ORDER

フ	ユ		

PRACTICE

ユ									

ユ

yu

as "you" in "youth," but shorter

ORIGIN   (YO 1873)

与	弓	ヨ	ヨ

STROKE ORDER

フ	ヲ	ヨ	

PRACTICE

ヨ									

ヨ

yo

as "Yo" in "York," but shorter

ラ

ra

as "ra" in "mirage," but shorter

ORIGIN　　　(RA/RYŌ 598)

良	ウ	ラ	ラ

STROKE ORDER

ー	ラ		

PRACTICE

リ

ri

as "ree" in "reek," but shorter

ORIGIN　　　(RI 596)

利	リ	り	

STROKE ORDER

l	リ		

PRACTICE

ORIGIN   (RU 409)

| 流 | ル | ノL | ル |

STROKE ORDER

| ノ | ル | | |

PRACTICE

ル									

ル

ru

as "ru" in "rule,"
but shorter

ORIGIN   (REI 413)

| 礼 | レ | レ | レ |

STROKE ORDER

| レ | | | |

PRACTICE

レ									

レ

re

as "re" in "red"

ロ

ro

as "ro" in "roar," but shorter

ORIGIN   (RO 256)

呂	ロ	ロ	

STROKE ORDER

l	ㄇ	ロ	

PRACTICE

ワ

wa

as "wa" in "watt"

ORIGIN   (WA 416)

和	ロ	ワ	ワ

STROKE ORDER

l	ワ		

PRACTICE

ヲ

ORIGIN   (KO, part of 856)

乎	ノ	シ	ヲ

STROKE ORDER

一	二	ヲ	

o

as "o" in "or," but shorter

PRACTICE

ン

ORIGIN   (NI)

尓	ヒ	ヒ	ン

STROKE ORDER

丶	ン		

n

as "n" in "sin"

PRACTICE

MINI REVIEW ナ ー ン / NA — N

heri   helicopter

へ り

memo   memo

メ モ

hire   fillet

ヒ レ

miruku   milk

ミ ル ク

kanū   canoe

カ ヌ ー

wanisu   varnish

ワ ニ ス

rōn   loan

ロ ー ン

naifu   knife

ナ イ フ

furē   Hooray!

フ レ ー

nōto   note, notebook

ノ ー ト

taiya   tire (car)

タ イ ヤ

kamera   camera

カ　メ　ラ

nēmu   name, reputation

ネ　ー　ム

yūmoa   humor

ユ　ー　モ　ア

mainasu   minus

マ　イ　ナ　ス

sararī   salary

サ　ラ　リ　ー

hanmā   hammer

ハ　ン　マ　ー

yōyō   yoyo

ヨ　ー　ヨ　ー

hankachi   handkerchief

ハ　ン　カ　チ

yunīku   unique

ユ　ニ　ー　ク

nekutai   necktie

ネ　ク　タ　イ

hōmuran   home run

ホ　ー　ム　ラ　ン

VOICED AND HALF-VOICED SOUNDS

ga   as "ga" in "garden" but shorter

ガ

gi   as "gee" in "geese" but shorter

ギ

gu   as "goo" in "goose" but shorter

グ

ge   as "ge" in "get"

ケ

go   as "go" in "gore" but shorter

ゴ

za   as "za" in "bizarre" but shorter

ザ

ji   as "jee" in "jeep" but shorter

ジ

zu   as "zoo" but shorter

ズ

ze   as "ze" in "zest"

ゼ

zo   as "zo" in "Azores" but shorter

ゾ

da   as "da" in "dark" but shorter

ダ													

ji   as "jee" in "jeep" but shorter

チ													

zu   as "zoo" but shorter

ツ													

de   as "de" in "desk"

テ													

do   as "doo" in "door" but shorter

ド													

ba   as "ba" in "bark" but shorter   *pa*   as "pa" in "park" but shorter

バ						パ							

bi   as "bea" in "beak" but shorter   *pi*   as "pea" in "peak" but shorter

ビ						ピ							

bu   as "boo" in "boot" but shorter   *pu*   as "poo" in "pool" but shorter

ブ						プ							

be   as "be" in "beg"   *pe*   as "pe" in "peg"

ベ						ペ							

bo   as "bo" in "bore" but shorter   *po*   as "po" in "pork" but shorter

ボ				ポ				

REVIEW OF VOICED AND HALF-VOICED SOUNDS

biru   office building

ビル

zero   zero

ゼロ

basu   bus, bath

バス

giya   gear

ギャ

dansu   dance

ダンス

gēmu   game

ゲーム

gaido   guide, guidebook

ガイド

gorufu   golf

ゴルフ

bēsu   base

ベース

zubon   trousers

ズボン

gorira   gorilla

ゴリラ

daburu — double
ダブル

zōn — zone
ゾーン

jiguzagu — zigzag
ジグザグ

repōto — report
レポート

jīnzu — jeans
ジーンズ

wāpuro — word processor
ワープロ

pachinko — Japanese pinball
パチンコ

dezāto — dessert
デザート

pīman — green pepper
ピーマン

mai pēsu — at one's own speed ("my pace")
マイペース

arubaito — part-time job
アルバイト

COMBINED SOUNDS KYA—RYO / キャ — リョ

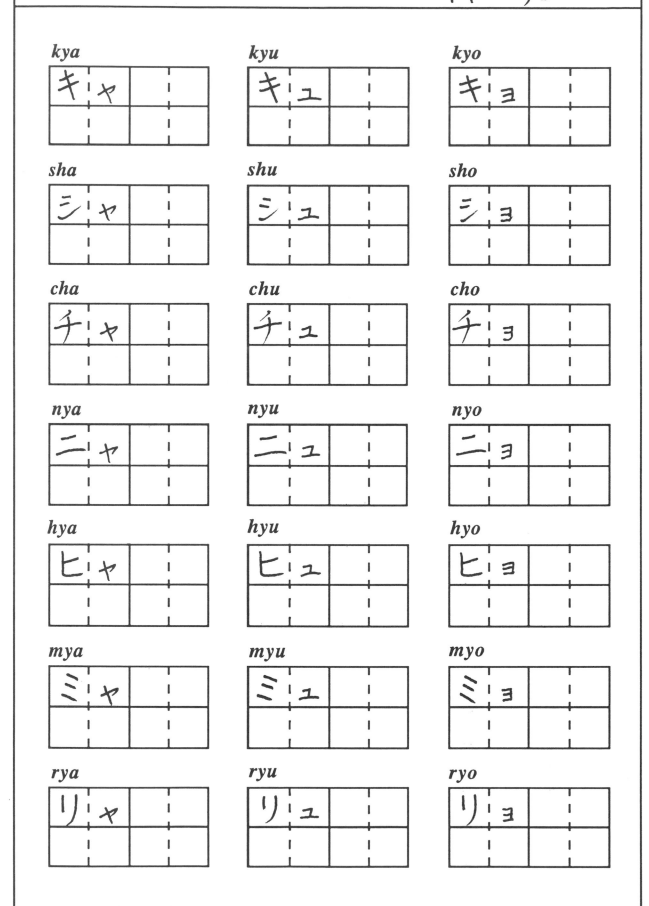

VOICED COMBINED SOUNDS GYA—BYO / ギャ—ビョ

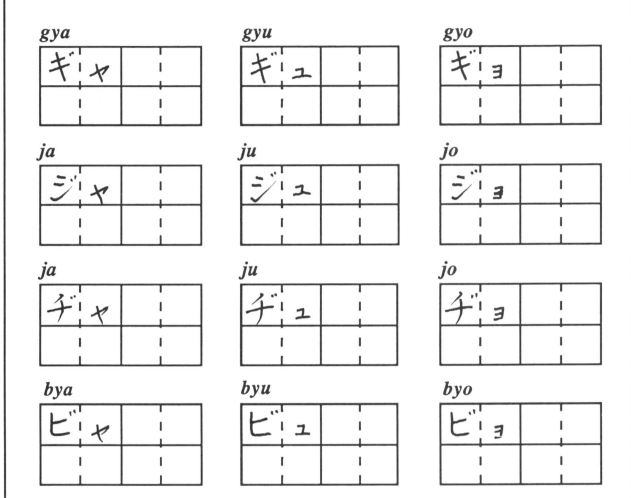

gya	gyu	gyo
ギャ	ギュ	ギョ

ja	ju	jo
ジャ	ジュ	ジョ

ja	ju	jo
ヂャ	ヂュ	ヂョ

bya	byu	byo
ビャ	ビュ	ビョ

HALF-VOICED COMBINED SOUNDS PYA—PYO / ピャ—ピョ

pya	pyu	pyo
ピャ	ピュ	ピョ

REVIEW OF COMBINED SOUNDS AND DOUBLE CONSONANTS

shō   show

ショー

netto   net

ネット

fan   fan (sports)

ファン

yeti   yeti

イェティ

nyūsu   news

ニュース

fōku   fork; folk

フォーク

chekku   check

チェック

jerī   jelly

ジェリー

chōku   chalk

チョーク

wotchi   watch

ウォッチ

disuku   disk

ディスク

fairu   file

ファイル

wēbu/wēvu   wave (hair)

ウェーヴ

bideo/video   video

ヴィデオ

manshon   apartment house

マンション

windō   window

ウィンドー

mājan   mahjong

マージャン

wētā   waiter

ウェーター

kyasshu   cash

キャッシュ

hyūman   human

ヒューマン

pitchā   pitcher (sports)

ピッチャー

duetto   duet

デュエット

REVIEW THROUGH INTERNATIONAL PLACE NAMES

Ajia Asia

アジア

Suisu Switzerland

スイス

Rōma Rome

ローマ

Kanada Canada

カナダ

Doitsu Germany

ドイツ

Atene Athens

アテネ

Puraha Prague

プラハ

Amerika America

アメリカ

Oranda Holland

オランダ

Igirisu England

イギリス

Mekishiko Mexico

メキシコ

Mosukuwa Moscow

モ|ス|ク|ワ

Betonamu Vietnam

ベ|ト|ナ|ム

Shidonī Sydney

シ|ド|ニ|ー

Kyūba Cuba

キ|ュ|ー|バ

Wīn Vienna

ウ|ィ|ー|ン

Furansu France

フ|ラ|ン|ス

Yōroppa Europe

ヨ|ー|ロ|ッ|パ

Firipin Philippines

フ|ィ|リ|ピ|ン

Bagudaddo Baghdad

バ|グ|ダ|ッ|ド

Echiopia Ethiopia

エ|チ|オ|ピ|ア

Noruwē Norway

ノ|ル|ウ|ェ|ー

Jakaruta Jakarta

ジャカルタ

Sanchiago Santiago

サンチアゴ

Pōtsumasu Portsmouth

ポーツマス

Hariuddo Hollywood

ハリウッド

Myunhen Munich

ミュンヘン

Guatemara Guatemala

グァテマラ

Marusēyu Marseilles

マルセーユ

Betsurehemu Bethlehem

ベツレヘム

Dieppu Dieppe

ディエップ

Benechia/Venechia Venice

ヴェネチア

Chunijia/Tunijia Tunisia

テュニジア

III

FINAL REVIEW

FINAL REVIEW

ABOUT JAPAN
Copy each line in the space provided.

せかいちずをみましょう。にほ

んはアジアたいりくのひがしにあ

る、なんぼくにほそながいくにで

す。そのひろさはアメリカのカり

フォルニアしゅうとだいたいおな

じです。よっつのおもなしまにわ

かれています。いちばんおおきい

のは、ほんしゅうで、このしまの

まんなかへんにとうきょうがあり

ます。ふじさんという、うつくし

いやまもあります。にばんめにお

111

おきいしまは、いちばんきたにあるほっかいどうで、なつはすずしいですが、ふゆはさむくて、ゆきがたくさんふりますから、スキーやスケートができます。さんばんめにおおきいきゅうしゅうは、みなみにありますから、ふゆでもあたたかいです。よばんめのしこくは、きたのほうはみかんで、みなみのほうはさかなで、ゆうめいです。

FOOD ITEMS QUIZ

Fill in the blanks with appropriate romanization.

1. たまご _____ egg
2. パン _____ bread
3. コーヒー _____ coffee
4. かし _____ confectionery
5. ぶたにく _____ pork
6. ビール _____ beer
7. レモンティー _____ lemon tea
8. くだもの _____ fruit
9. しょうゆ _____ soy sauce
10. チーズ _____ cheese
11. バター _____ butter
12. オムレツ _____ omelette
13. やさい _____ vegetable
14. りんご _____ apple
15. ラーメン _____ Chinese noodles
16. ヨーグルト _____ yoghurt
17. さとう _____ sugar
18. ビスケット _____ biscuit
19. なっとう _____ fermented soybean
20. ジュース _____ juice
21. かずのこ _____ herring roe
22. プリン _____ custard pudding
23. みかん _____ mikan orange
24. パルフェ _____ parfait
25. ヴェニソン _____ venison

FLORA AND FAUNA QUIZ

Fill in the blanks with *hiragana* (H) or *katakana* (K) as appropriate.

1. inu (H) _____ dog
2. sakana (H) _____ fish
3. raion (K) _____ lion
4. take (H) _____ bamboo
5. kaede (H) _____ maple
6. yūkari (K) _____ eucalyptus
7. tsubaki (H) _____ camellia
8. chūrippu (K) _____ tulip
9. maguro (H) _____ tuna
10. koara (K) _____ koala bear
11. nihonzaru (H) _____ Japanese monkey
12. kangarū (K) _____ kangaroo
13. nezumi (H) _____ mouse, rat
14. ajisai (H) _____ hydrangea
15. haibisukasu (K) _____ hibiscus
16. hyō (H) _____ leopard
17. kānēshon (K) _____ carnation
18. kabutomushi (H) _____ Goliath beetle
19. hebi (H) _____ snake
20. pengin (K) _____ penguin
21. hirame (H) _____ flatfish
22. botan (H) _____ peony
23. mahoganī (K) _____ mahogany
24. suisen (H) _____ narcissus
25. ichō (H) _____ gingko

PERSONAL NAMES QUIZ

Underline the *kana* error in each name and write the correct version in the blank.

1. じろお	_____	Jiro (Jirō)
2. キャロル	_____	Carole (Kyaroru)
3. ねいこ	_____	Reiko
4. ノームン	_____	Norman (Nōman)
5. とるお	_____	Teruo
6. ウェソディー	_____	Wendy (Wendī)
7. まサよし	_____	Masayoshi
8. ヴァヌサ	_____	Vanessa (Vanesa)
9. おけみ	_____	Akemi
10. ドワート	_____	Dwight (Dowaito)
11. けんいし	_____	Kenichi (Ken'ichi)
12. シェーノ	_____	Shane (Shēn)
13. ゆきい	_____	Yukiko
14. チュリー	_____	Julie (Jurī)
15. おりへ	_____	Orie
16. ソウフィ	_____	Sophie (Sōfi)
17. っとむ	_____	Tsutomu
18. ウィリマム	_____	William (Wiriamu)
19. ひでミ	_____	Hidemi
20. ジャッタ	_____	Jack (Jakku)
21. されこ	_____	Sawako
22. デヴィッド	_____	David (Deviddo)
23. のそむ	_____	Nozomu
24. エリザペス	_____	Elizabeth (Erizabesu)
25. ラッセル	_____	Russell (Rasseru)

KANA WORD SEARCH

ヌ	カ	い	ル	イ	サ	ミ	ま	エ	ラ	ヤ	う	く	れ	プ
ご	う	ウ	り	め	ね	キ	な	ジ	こ	つ	ぞ	め	ロ	ぬ
モ	ぜ	な	ン	あ	ま	ウ	オ	け	と	わ	り	ぺ	ぼ	ぶ
よ	ね	ほ	る	ト	わ	ホ	に	ス	ぎ	さ	ラ	ど	す	し
ら	そ	し	ぷ	ネ	し	せ	ス	ど	ク	と	る	む	う	パ
い	わ	つ	め	ズ	う	ち	ま	テ	レ	ビ	か	ふ	べ	ぐ
ア	お	れ	ユ	で	ま	も	ざ	た	ル	ア	ん	シ	さ	か
よ	ろ	い	に	し	ワ	る	ネ	あ	に	ゾ	じ	い	ね	す
や	る	ば	ん	が	ル	ト	だ	ナ	か	ん	げ	も	ゴ	ケ
ず	み	き	メ	グ	ツ	ン	イ	て	し	ら	ち	デ	ニ	ム
の	プ	せ	ふ	ぐ	ラ	ロ	ハ	え	は	た	パ	ヌ	び	ち
デ	そ	レ	ぽ	ゆ	ン	フ	が	タ	ポ	ソ	え	つ	ノ	む
ザ	て	お	ゼ	モ	き	ん	レ	る	コ	ひ	の	き	ろ	ま
イ	た	や	ゆ	ン	お	ン	け	ン	リ	ソ	ガ	み	ヒ	お
ン	く	へ	マ	ス	ト	ぬ	エ	ノ	み	つ	ヨ	こ	い	か

Find the fifty words below in the square above, moving in a straight line in any direction including diagonals. The first thirty words are in *hiragana,* the rest *katakana.* (We found over 200 other *hiragana* words, most of two symbols and not found elsewhere in this book. How many can you find? Fifty or more means you have a good vocabulary.)

* * * * *

madogiwazoku (staff passed over for promotion), *tsuridōgu* (fishing gear), *haragei* (non-verbal communication), *shitsurei* (rudeness), *kanji* (character), *fugu* (blowfish), *hinoki* (cypress), *kanemochi* (rich person), *ganbaru* (try your best), *daruma* (Buddha doll), *yuki* (snow), *tate* (verticality), *oya* (parent), *uchi* (home, inner group), *sewa* (care), *ongaeshi* (repayment of favor), *tsukimi* (moon viewing), *umeboshi* (pickled plum), *nemawashi* (behind-the-scenes maneuvering), *musubu* (bind), *nukeru* (be missing), *furusato* (hometown), *ame* (rain), *hosoi* (slender), *kaiko* (silkworm), *heta* (unskilled), *tanin* (stranger), *yoroi* (armor), *nama* (raw), *mizu* (water); *nairon, kiosuku, gurafu, dezain, terebi, hosuteru, warutsu, gasorin, furonto, puropera, purezento, kaunto, pasokon, misairu, tarento, rajio, gomu, masuto, denimu, yoga.* (Look up the *katakana* words you don't know.)

QUIZ ANSWERS

	Food items	Flora/fauna	Names
1.	tamago	いぬ	じろう
2.	pan	さかな	キャロル
3.	kōhī	ライオン	れいこ
4.	kashi	たけ	ノーマン
5.	butaniku	かえで	てるお
6.	bīru	ユーカリ	ウェンディー
7.	remon tī	つばき	まさよし
8.	kudamono	チューリップ	ヴァネサ
9.	shōyu	まぐろ	あけみ
10.	chīzu	コアラ	ドワイト
11.	batā	にほんざる	けんいち
12.	omuretsu	カンガルー	シェーン
13.	yasai	ねずみ	ゆき
14.	ringo	あじさい	ジュリー
15.	rāmen	ハイビスカス	おりえ
16.	yōguruto	ひょう	ソーフィ
17.	satō	カーネーション	つとむ
18.	bisuketto	かぶとむし	ウィリアム
19.	nattō	へび	ひでみ
20.	jūsu	ペンギン	ジャック
21.	kazunoko	ひらめ	さわこ
22.	purin	ぼたん	デヴィッド
23.	mikan	マホガニー	のぞむ
24.	parufe	すいせん	エリザベス
25.	benison/venison	いちょう	ラッセル

ENGLISH VERSION OF "ABOUT JAPAN"

Let's look at an atlas. Japan is a long, thin country lying on a north-south axis to the east of the Asian mainland. It's about the same size as the state of California in America. It consists of four main islands. The largest is Honshu, with Tokyo at its midpoint. The beautiful Mount Fuji is also found on this island. The next largest is Hokkaido, the northernmost island. Summer here is cool, and in winter heavy snow makes skiing and skating possible. Kyushu, the third largest island, lies to the south, so it's warm here even in winter. The fourth largest, Shikoku, is noted for mikan oranges from its northern half and fish from the south.

DO-IT-YOURSELF *KANA* CHARTS

Fill in the following charts, writing *hiragana* in the left part of each box and *katakana* in the right. Then check your entries against the charts in the Explanation of *Kana*.

Basic Kana Symbols

VOWELS

	a	i	u	e	o
	a	i	u	e	o
k	ka	ki	ku	ke	ko
s	sa	shi	su	se	so
t	ta	chi	tsu	te	to
n	na	ni	nu	ne	no
h	ha	hi	fu	he	ho
m	ma	mi	mu	me	mo
y	ya		yu		yo
r	ra	ri	ru	re	ro
w	wa				wo
n	n				

CONSONANTS

Basic Voiced Sounds

	a	i	u	e	o
g	ga	gi	gu	ge	go
z/j	za	ji	zu	ze	zo
d/z/j	da	ji	zu	de	do
b	ba	bi	bu	be	bo
p	pa	pi	pu	pe	po

Basic Combinations

	a	u	o
ky	kya	kyu	kyo
sh	sha	shu	sho
ch	cha	chu	cho
ny	nya	nyu	nyo
hy	hya	hyu	hyo
my	mya	myu	myo
ry	rya	ryu	ryo

Voiced Combinations

	a	u	o
gy	gya	gyu	gyo
j	ja	ju	jo
j	ja	ju	jo
by	bya	byu	byo
py	pya	pyu	pyo

119

THE *IROHA* VERSE

The *iroha* verse was written about a thousand years ago. Though based upon a teaching of Buddhism its main use is for writing practice, for it includes all of the *kana* symbols with the exception of the final *n* (ん). In ancient times *mu* (む) was used where ん is used today. The order of symbols in the verse — particularly the first half dozen — is important because it is still sometimes followed in listings, in similar fashion to the English order "a, b, c."

Try copying out the verse in the space at the foot of the page.

いろはにほへど　　ちりぬるを
わがよたれぞ　　　つねならむ
うゐのおくやま　　けふこえて
あさきゆめみじ　　ゑひもせず

The modern romanized version is: *Iro wa nioedo chirinuru o / Waga yo tare zo tsune naran / Ui no okuyama kyō koete / Asaki yume miji ei mo sezu.*

A literal paraphrase is: "Colors are fragrant, but they fade away. In this world of ours none lasts forever. Today cross the high mountain of life's illusions [i.e., rise above this physical world], and there will be no more shallow dreaming, no more drunkenness [i.e., there will be no more uneasiness, no more temptations]."

The above translation is given in the appendices of the *Japanese - English Character Dictionary* (edited by A. Nelson, published by Charles E. Tuttle Company, 1962). Readers who wish to learn more about the historical use of *kana*, such as けふ for the modern きょう, are recommended to consult this work.

125

129

132

134